The Louvre

Pierre Quoniam
Inspecteur général des musées de France

LE LOUVRE

Translation:
C. de Chabannes

Editions des musées nationaux, Paris

ISBN 2.7118.0040.7

Pierre Quoniam
Inspecteur général des musées de France

LE LOUVRE

Translation:
C. de Chabannes

Editions des musées nationaux, Paris

ISBN 2.7118.0040.7

Plan
of the Louvre Museum

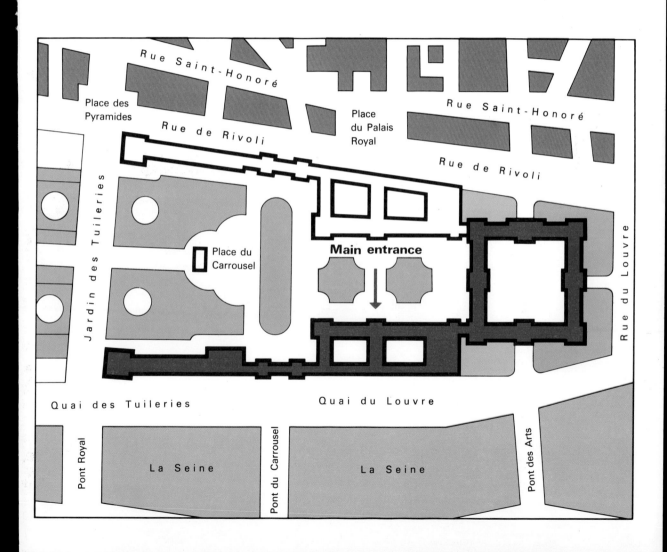

Rue Saint-Honoré

Place des
Pyramides

Rue de Rivoli

Place
du Palais
Royal

Rue Saint-Honoré

Rue de Rivoli

Jardin des Tuileries

Place du
Carrousel

Main entrance

Rue du Louvre

Quai des Tuileries

Quai du Louvre

Pont Royal

La Seine

Pont du Carrousel

La Seine

Pont des Arts

Ground Floor

Egyptian antiquities

Greco-Roman antiquities

Oriental antiquities

Sculptures

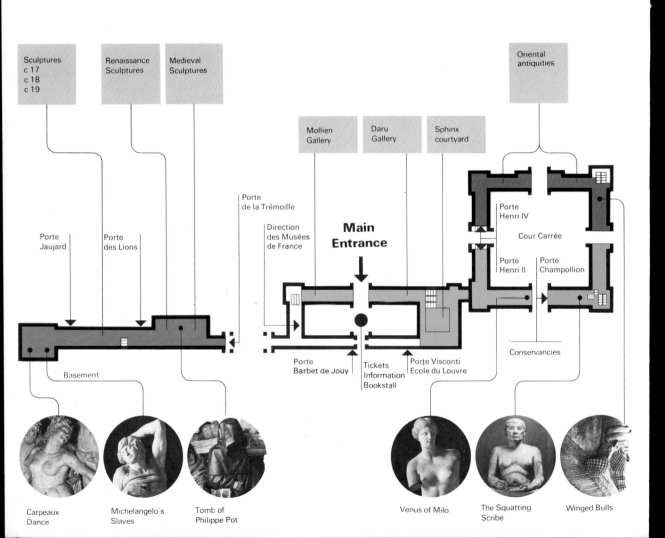

Sculptures
c 17
c 18
c 19

Renaissance
Sculptures

Medieval
Sculptures

Oriental
antiquities

Mollien
Gallery

Daru
Gallery

Sphinx
courtyard

Porte
de la Trémoille

Direction
des Musées
de France

**Main
Entrance**

Porte
Henri IV

Cour Carrée

Porte
Jaujard

Porte
des Lions

Porte
Henri II

Porte
Champollion

Basement

Porte
Barbet de Jouy

Tickets
Information
Bookstall

Porte Visconti
Ecole du Louvre

Conservancies

Carpeaux
Dance

Michelangelo's
Slaves

Tomb of
Philippe Pot

Venus of Milo

The Squatting
Scribe

Winged Bulls

Art Objects

Gallery of Drawings

Paintings

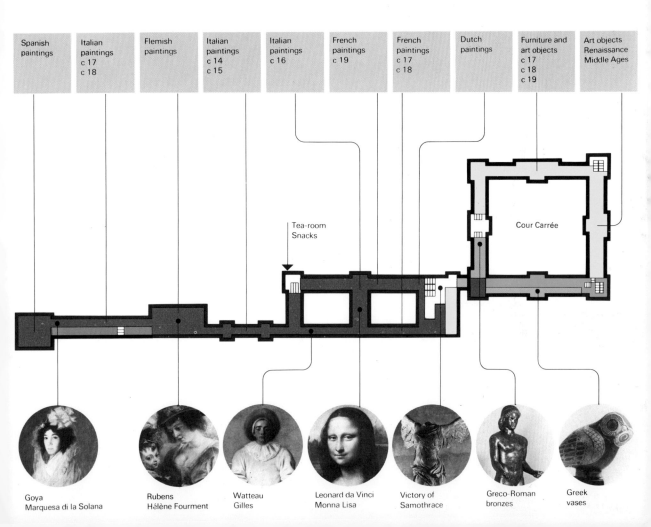

| Spanish paintings | Italian paintings c 17 c 18 | Flemish paintings | Italian paintings c 14 c 15 | Italian paintings c 16 | French paintings c 19 | French paintings c 17 c 18 | Dutch paintings | Furniture and art objects c 17 c 18 c 19 | Art objects Renaissance Middle Ages |

Tea-room
Snacks

Cour Carrée

Goya
Marquesa di la Solana

Rubens
Hélène Fourment

Watteau
Gilles

Leonard da Vinci
Monna Lisa

Victory of
Samothrace

Greco-Roman
bronzes

Greek
vases

Second Floor

Gallery of Drawings

Paintings

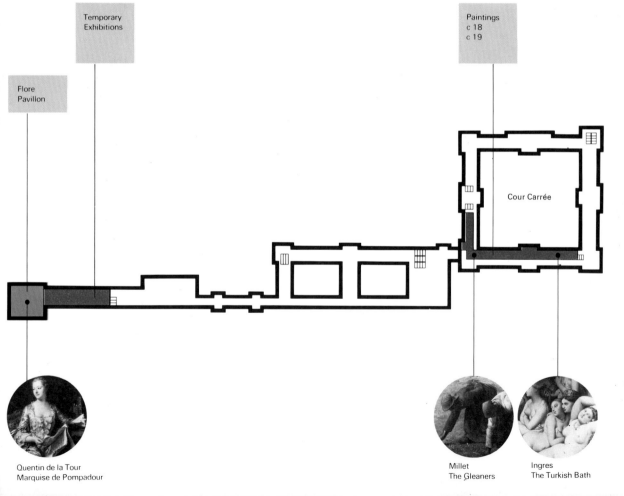

Temporary
Exhibitions

Paintings
c 18
c 19

Flore
Pavillon

Cour Carrée

Quentin de la Tour
Marquise de Pompadour

Millet
The Gleaners

Ingres
The Turkish Bath

© Éditions des musées nationaux, Paris   Maquette Frutiger & Pfäffli   Imprimerie moderne du Lion, Paris

The Palace and Museum of the Louvre

This was originally a Mediaeval fortress, built under Philippe August in 1200 at the point where the defences of Paris were weakest, on the site known as "Lupara", which became "Louvre" in French. This corresponds to the present site of the South-West quarter of the Square Courtyard. When it ceased to serve as a defence post, Charles V (1364-1380) had it enlarged and adapted for use as a royal residence. However, its new function soon came to an end; the vicissitudes of the Hundred Years War, then the attraction of the Loire Valley diverted the attention of the sovereigns from their capital for over one and a half centuries.

When they returned to Paris, the old fortified castle was abolished. François I had its imposing keep demolished in 1527, then in 1546, he decided to replace the rest by a building in the Renaissance style. The operation was entrusted to the architect Pierre Lescot, who completed it under the last Valois kings and is supposed to have drawn up the plans of the new palace. In any case, the work was carried on during the following reigns and centuries in the same spirit of classical regularity.

Catherine de Medicis then ordered Philibert Delorme and Jean Bulland to construct two galleries, about 500 meters to the West, on the spot known as the Tuileries, in order to connect the partly transformed Louvre with the palace built at the same period. These are the *Small* and the *Great Galleries*, the latter also being known as the "Gallery by the Water", recalling the name of Henri IV (1589-1610). During the 17th century, under Louis XIII, then Louis XIV, the remaining buildings surrounding the present *Square Courtyard* were raised by Lemercier, then by Le Vau. They are flanked on the East by Perrault's Colonnade (1).

In the early 19th century, under Napoleon Ist, Percier and Fontaine began to construct the North Wing, symetrical to the Great Gallery, at the same time as they completed the quadrilateral buildings and their decoration. Half a century later, Napoleon III ordered Visconti, then Lefuel, to construct the buildings bordering the *Napoleon Courtyard* on the North and South, so as to complete the enclosure of the space between the Old Louvre and the Tuileries (2). However, the Tuileries were destroyed by fire in 1871

1. The Louvre Palace:
Perrault's Colonnade

and the unity of the huge palatial ensemble was destroyed on the west. Only the two corner pavilions of Marsan (on the side of the rue de Rivoli) and Flore (on the side of the Seine) were restored.

Though the Louvre Museum was born only at the end of the 18th century, during the French Revolution, the idea had been launched forty years earlier. In a pamphlet against the secret of the royal collections, Lafont de Saint-Yenne had suggested that these should be exhibited to the public in the Great Gallery of the palace. In response to this wish, which was taken up by other writers and philosophers, and notably by Diderot in *L'Encyclopaedie* (article "Louvre", 1765), a first project was submitted, unsuccessfully, to Louis XV by the Marquis de Marigny, Director of Buildings. The idea was taken up again under Louis XVI and studied attentively by Comte d'Angiviller, Marigny's successor. However, it came to nothing because of financial difficulties and political events.

The Convention must be given the credit of realizing it after the fall of the Monarchy. The "Central Museum of Arts" was instituted by decree on July 27th 1793 and inaugurated on August 10th of that year. This opening, however, was partial and temporary. The Great Gallery, where the paintings were exhibited, and the ground floor of the Small Gallery, given over to antiquities, were fitted up progressively through the whole revolutionary and imperial period, especially after 1802, when Vivant Denon became Director General of the Museum. The establishment was constantly enriched by objects brough back from the wars and was baptised Napoleon Museum in 1803, when it presented what was probably the most splendid collection of masterpieces of all time.

This was dispersed in 1815 by the restitutions imposed by the Allies after the fall of Napoleon. However, the Louvre collections were again rapidly increased under the Restoration and the July Monarchy, notably through the transfer to the palace of part of the sculptures from the Museum of French Monuments, closed in 1817, and through the continual development of the departments of Greek, Roman, Egyptian and Oriental antiquities. Thus the Museum gradually spread into the four wings of the Square Courtyard.

The Second Empire saw the construction of the wing with the Denon Pavilion in the middle and the three buildings connecting it transversely with the Great Gallery. These provided new rooms and a visiting circuit better adapted to the number and diversity of the works exhibited. Constant alterations and re-alterations of the installations were carried out as the science of museology developed, together with the history of art and archeology. Others were necessitated by the constant increase in the collections and the need for to improve the reception of the ever-swelling flood of visitors (nearly three million per year at present). The contemporary period saw an important extension when the Flore wing and pavilion were opened to the public in 1968. Thus the Louvre Museum now spreads over three fifths of the palace whose name it bears, the rest being occupied by the Ministry of Finance and the Museum of Decorative Arts.

Its collections are divided among six departments: Oriental Antiquities, Egyptian Antiquities, Greek and Roman Antiquities; Paintings, Sculptures and Art Objects—to which must be added small Gallery a of Drawings.

2. The Louvre under Napoleon III:
The Denon pavillion

3. The Mediaeval Louvre:
detail of the "altar-piece of the Paris Parliament"
(mid 15th century)

Oriental Antiquities

The department of Oriental Antiquities, installed in the northern half of the ground-floor of the buildings in the Square Courtyard, presents an almost complete panorama of the ancient civilisations of Asia. This department was created in 1881 and its history is closely linked with the development of archeological research in Mesopotania, Iran, the countries of the Levant and Cyprus, as well as in Punic North Africa. Beginning with Paul-Emile Botta's excavations in Khorsabad in 1843, the products of which came to found the Louvre's first "Assyrian Museum" in 1847—they extend to the contemporary findings of Claude Schaeffer at Ras-Shamra and André Parrot at Mari, and include notably the discoveries of the Renan Mission in Palestine and Syria (1860), of the Delegation to Persia, directed from 1897 on by Jacques de Morgan, and of the French archeologists who explored the site of Tello in Lower Mesopotania between 1877 and 1933 and brought back the revelation of the Sumerian civilisation.

The section dedicated to ancient Mesopotania, Sumer and Akkad is especially rich. This period is illustrated by important monuments, such as *Vulture Stele*, raised in 2450 by Eannatelle, prince of Lagash, in memory of his conquests, or the no less famous one raised about 2270 by *Naramsin*, ruler of Agada, to commemorate his victory over the barbarians of of the Zagros mountains on the borders of Iran. A masterly composition shows him as a god, striding up the wooded mountain and trampling his adverseries under foot (4). Several representations of this prince of Lagash bear witness to the Sumerian renaissance at the end of the third millenary, during the reign of the *ensi Gudea*. One of them, in calcite, shows him holding a vase, attribute of his divinity, from which gush life-giving waters full of fishes (6). Finally, there are numerous objects—cylindric seals, inscribed tablets, ornaments, weapons, vases, frescos and sculptures—discovered at Mari and testifying to ten centuries of

its history (28th to 18th centuries BC). In the room reserved for this city and for Larsa we find an alabaster statuette, a masterpiece of Sumerian art, dating from about 2500 BC. It was dedicated by the *intendant Ebih-il* (5) to the goddess Ishtar. The praying figure is seated on a wickerwork stool, wearing a sheepskin skirt. The incrusted eyes lend intense life to the face, and this is accentuated by the half-smile that seems to float on his lips.

One object which is a work of art as well as an historical document stands out in this department, and indeed in the Louvre Museum, testifying better than any other to the grandure of the first Babylonian

4. Stele of Naram-Sin, king of Agadia (ap.2270 BC)

5. Ebih-il, intendant of Mari (ap.2500 BC)

6. Gudea with gushing vase
(ap. 2150 BC)

kingdom. This is the *Code of King Hammurabi* (1792-1750 BC), discovered in 1901 at Susa, where it had been brought as loot during the 12th century BC. This conical cylinder of hard, black stone is 2,25 meters high and covered with cuniform characters, in the Akkadian language, it constitutes not so much a "code" as a compilation of common law, of exemplary phrases dictated by the King "so that his country might learn firm discipline and right conduct". At the top, a majestic scene shows Hammurabi standing in prayer before Shamash, god of the Sun and of Justice. The remains which testify to the might of Assyria from the 9th to the 7th century BC have a dramatic quality. Great bas-reliefs—elements of the decoration of the palaces of Nimrud, Ninena and above all Khorsabad—evoke the glorious deeds of the Kings who raised these vast buildings, especially those of *Sargon II* (721-705 BC) represented in his function as supreme Administrator, giving instructions to his minister (8). Huge sculptures suggest the immensity of the palace raised by order of this king at Khorsabad: *winged bulls with human heads* 4 meters high—guardian spirits watching over the entrance to the throne room, together with lion-taming giants (10).

Other collections illustrate the civilisations which flourished East of Mesopotania, on the plateau to which the invading Iranians gave their name at the end of the 2nd millenary, and at the foot of this plateau. Here are painted ceramics, vases in the form of animals, praying statuettes from the region of archaic Susa, from the 6th millenary to the middle of the 4th. Elamite works such as the *Smiling God*, in bronze and originally entirely coated over with gold, show the influence of Mesopotania over the kingdom of Susa during the 3rd and 2nd millenaries; others, like the huge capital decorated with half-length bulls (9) shich surmounted one of the columns of the palace of Darius (521-485) at Susa, testify to the grandure of the Achemenide kingdom of Persia. From the same

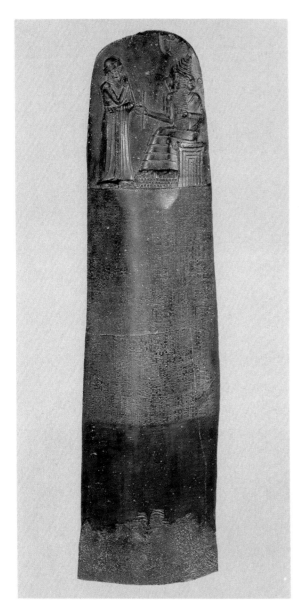

building comes the panel of enamelled bricks representing the *Archers of the Guard*, the "Immortals" (13), the pick of the magnificent army that defeated the Greeks at Marathon. Here are Parthian terracottas (200 BC-300 AD), inspired by Hellenic art, and sumptuous pieces from the Sassanide period (224-651) lake this applied ornament in the form of a *royal bust* from the end of the 6th century (11) which reflect, on the contrary, the vigourous renewal of Irananism on the eve of the Arab conquest.

Numerous objects in bronze from civilisations in this area, reveal the originality of the art of the high valleys of Luristan, on the eastern edge of the Iranian plateau, from the middle of the 3rd millenium to the 7th century BC: arms, "standards", hatchets and votive pins, plaques from horses' bits (12), decorated with geniis, animals or stylised monsters.

This review ends with antiquities from the Levantine countries. Numerous objects come from Palestine, the essentially biblical land, certain of them, disovered in the Negeb, dating back to the 4th millenary. Here are several monuments from the Syro-Phenician region: certain date from the Roman period, such as the Mithreum of Sidon or the fine

8. Sargon II of Assyria and his Minister (end of 8th century BC)

7. Code of Hammurabi, king of Babylone (1792-1750 BC)

ensemble of Palmyrian sculptures; others are contemporary with the Persian domination, like the sarcophaguses from Sidon (5th-4th centuries BC) which bear the unmistakeable mark of the double influence of Egypt and Ionia; yet others belong to high antiquity, such as the supremely precious pieces discovered at Byblos and above all at Ras-Shamra, the ancient Ugarit, the point where the Syrian, Egyptian and Mycenian civilisations met during the 2nd millenary (14). The no-less complicated history of Cyprus, from the early Bronze Age (2300-2000) to the 3rd century BC is illustrated by an abundant series of vases, terracotta figurines (16), jewels and sculptures, while the Punic and Libico-Punic monuments brought from Tunisia and Algeria evoke the distant prolongations of the Phenician civilisation.

A section of Islamic Art is attached to the department of Oriental Antiquities, but for the moment, only part of this collection is on exhibit. Most of the objects come from Egypt, Syria and Persia: ceramics, materials, carpets, objects in metal-work, such as the copper bowl encrusted with silver and gold, originating from Egypt or Syria, known as the St. Louis Baptistery (about 1300) (15).

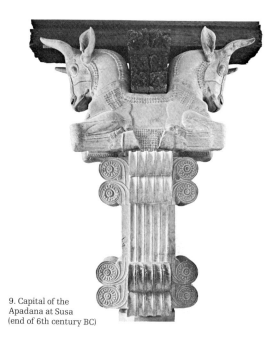

9. Capital of the Apadana at Susa (end of 6th century BC)

10. Assyrian winged bull, Khorsabad (8th century BC)

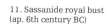

11. Sassanide royal bust (ap. 6th century BC)

12. Plaque from a Luristan bit (8th century BC)

14. Gold peg, known as "The Hunt", Ras-Shamra (14th century BC)

13. Archers of the Guard of Darius I (521-485 BC) Susa

15. Moslem art: "Baptistery of St. Louis"
(about 1300)

16. Mother and Child,
Cypriot idol (ap.2000 BC)

13

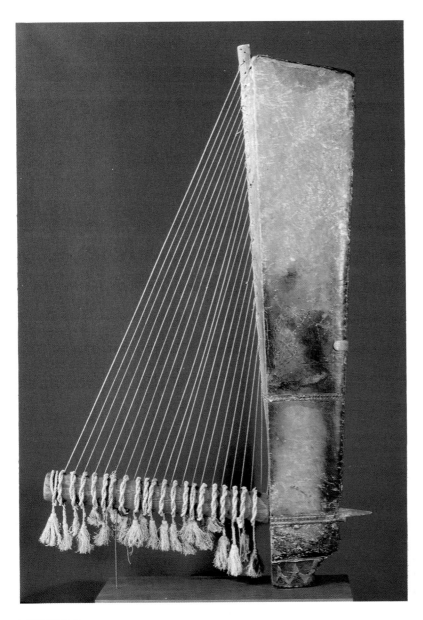

17. Trigonal harp,
Saïte period (7th–6th cens BC)

Egyptian Antiquities

Another department world-famous in the field of archeology, but of earlier creation (1826) than the precedent, is the department of Egyptian Antiquities. It has been continually enriched by donations and purchases, while a number of French scientists, beginning with its founder and first curator, Jean-François Champollion, have contributed their discoveries. Today, its collections make it possible to follow the civilisation and art of ancient Egypt throughout the whole continuity of their evolution, from their origins to the Christian era. They are exhibited on the ground floor of the South-East quarter of the Square Courtyard buildings, on the so-called "Egyptian Staircase" and on the first floor of the South Wing, in a series of rooms overlooking the courtyard. These rooms are known as the "Charles X Museum" on account of the decorations executed in 1827-1833 which confer on it an historical interest worthy of respect.

For many, the chief attraction of this department lies in the exceptionally rich documentation on the life and custom of the ancient inhabitants of the Nile Valley. These are illustrated by innumerable texts, pictural representations, and all kinds of everyday objects (weapons, tools, recipients, furniture, clothes, toilet articles, jewels, games, toys, accessories used by the scribes, muscial instruments, etc. (17, 23, 30, 32). The majority of visitors however are chiefly interested in the brilliant series of masterpieces, some of which count among the most famous in Egyptian art.

The first manifestation of this art is illustrated by the Gebel-el-Arak knife (about 3400 BC), with its ivory handle decorated with scenes of war and hunting (18). Here we see the influence of Asia, predominant during the predynastic era. It was during the Thinite period, under the two first dynasties, that Egyptian sculpture took on its own, original style, attaining a high technical level by the first centuries of the third millenary. A striking example is a limestone

monument, dating from about the year 3000 BC, brought from the royal necropolis at Abydos: the *stele* of King Ouadji, the so-called *Serpent-King* (19). It is decorated soberly and majestically with a representation of the façade of the king's palace, with a vertical projection of its walls. Surmounting it is a guardian falcon, bird of the god Horus incarnating the Egyptian dynasty. In the interiour we see the serpent whose coils inscribe the name of the King.

The creations of this archaic era, the works of Ancient Egypt (2778-2300)—sculpted in stone or wood; statues or bas-reliefs—are characterised by their grandure. This grandure was completed under the IVth and Vth dynasties, by a vigourous realism which gives a look of unmistakeable veracity to the specimens in the Louvre. Specially evident in the head of king Didoufri, executed in pink quartzite and which was probably part of a sphinx (20, or, in spite of mutilation it has undergone, in the moving group carved in wood of a Memphire functionary and his wife (21), this tendency to express intensely the personality of the individual portrayed is found in one

19. Serpent-King stele,
Thinite period (ap.3000 BC)

20. Head of King Didoufri,
Old Empire (ap.2600 BC)

of the most famous works of ancient Egypt: the *Squatting Scribe* (24). This painted limestone statuette was discored at Sakkara, in the chapel on a Vth dynasty tomb and possibly figures an administrator of the province known as Kaï. There is another statue from the same tomb in the department. Whether or not he is anonymous, the personnage, holding his quill and with the papyrus spread on his knees, fascinates us with his expressive physionomy, his eyes sparkling with intelligence, fixed attentively on the person who dictates to him. The impression is heightened by the incrustations of the eyes (opaque white quartz for the cornea, rock-crystal for the iris and ebony for the pupil). Other examples are the head in painted limestone of a man of Mongol type with shaven skull (20) and—in spite of the mutilations it has undergone—the moving group carved in wood, of a Memphite official and his wife (21).

The Middle Empire (2060-1785) under the XIth and XIIth dynasties, still aimed at realism, but a tendency to idealisation set in. This is demonstrated by two pieces in our collections: the rigid yet harmonious red sandstone statue of Amenemhatankh, "Chief of the Prophets" (22) and that in struccoed, painted wood of the graceful "Woman with Offerings", with her slender, elongated body, delicately modeller under the transparent tunic covered with a netting of pearls.

The tendency towards increasingly subtle idealisation finally took shape under the New Empire (1580-1085 BC), an incomparably glorious and prosperous period in the history of the Nile Valley. The absolute power of the Pharaohs, the brilliant life at Court, the wealth of the ruling class, gave rise to a truly "classic" art which best expressed the Egyptian peoples ideal of beauty. Grandure and nobility are tempered in this aesthetic with grace and gentleness. It is not easy to choose between all the masterpieces in the department which testify to this evolution. Many visitors are attracted by the greenstone statue of *Nephthys* (26) inscribed with the name of Amenophis III (1405-1370). The figure of the goddess is represented with sober elegance, standing, pressing a papyriform sceptre against her body. A bas-relief in painted limestone, taken from the tomb of Sethi I (1318-1298) in the Valley of the Kings, is another attraction. It shows the goddess Hathor, wearing a marvellous tunic, holding out to the sovereign her necklace charged with protective fluide (27). Here we find one of the finest examples of the sensibility and charm of the art of this period.

A work situated chronologically between the two cited above is thus all the more surprising: the extraordinary bust in red sandstone of Amenophis IV Akhenaton (1370-1352), offered by Egypt to France in gratitude for the part played by the latter in saving the monuments of Nubia (28). Here we see the result of a brief revolution, expressed in art as well as in religion by an extreme naturalism. The huge head is sculpted so as to be seen from below—its summit is 4 meters

21. Memphite official and his wife, Ancient Empire (ap.2500 BC)

22. Amenemhatankh, "Chief of the Prophets", Middle Empire (ap.1850 BC)

23. Stele of Antef,
high official of
Thoutmosis III
(1504–1450)

24. Squatting Scribe,
Ancient Empire
(ap.2500 BC)

above ground—and is typical of the official statuary of El Amarna, the new and ephemeral capital of the kingdom. Here is an art animated by a deeply introspective realism, which is not afraid to exagerate even to commit excesses in order to reveal the intense spiritual life of the "Seer" of Aton.

Other fine quality works illustrate the efforts of Egyptian sculptors under the last native dynasties to revive the realism of the art of the Old Empire. An elegant wooden statue from the XXXth dynasty (378-341) is specially characteristic of this archaistic tendency, associated with a stylistic elongation of the body. It represents a man standing, wearing a long tunic and whose shaven head shows that the exercised some priestly function (29).

The last days of Ancient Egypt—the Ptolemaic, Roman and Byzantine periods—are also represented in the Louvre by numerous series of antiquities.

26. The goddess Nephthys,
New Empire (ap.1400 BC)

25. "Woman with Offerings",
Middle Empire (ap.2000 BC)

28. Amenophis IV
Akhenaton (1370-1352 BC)

29. Anonymous priest, wood,
Late Period (4th cen.BC)

27. The goddess Hathor
protecting Sethi I,
New Empire (ap.1300 BC)

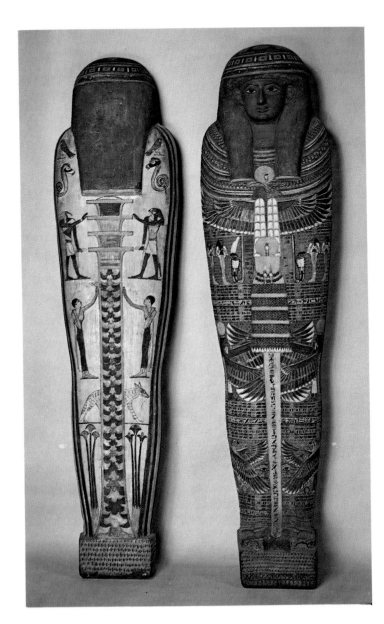

30. Sarcophagus (vat and lid)
of the Chancellor Imeneminet (6th cen.BC)

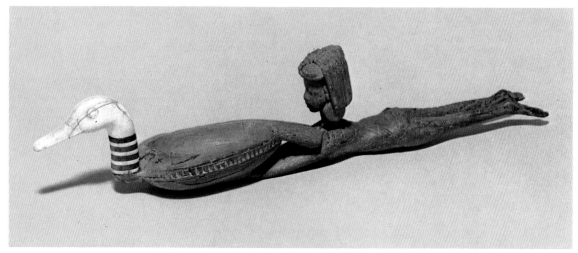

32. Cosmetics spoon of the "Swimming Woman" type (15th cen.BC)

31. Christ protecting the Abbot Mena (7th cen.AD)

Coptic art is so richly represented that we have been able to consecrate an entire section to it. Pieces of architecture, stonework reliefs, statuettes, wax-colour portraits, funeral masks, painted canvases, dalmatics, liturgical bronzes, ivories, glassware, ceramics reveal successively the Pharaonic and Hellenistic sources of this art from its beginnings in the 3rd century AD, its zenith during the Christian era (from the 4th century) and finally, after the Arab conquest (641), its prolongation up to the 12th century. The Coptic collections have now been rearranged in such a way that it has been possible partially to reconstruct from elements of its internal and external decoration, a church built in the 6th century and utilised at least till the 9th—that of the monastery of Saint-Apollo, at Baouït, a village in Middle Egypt. An extremely beautiful "ikon" from the monastery chapel—Christ protecting the abbot Mena (superior of the covent (7th cen.AD) (31)—has been placed near the upright beam of the triumphal arch.

Greek and Roman Antiquities

The third archeological department derives from the "Museum of Antiquities" opened in the Louvre in 1800. To the royal collections in this first foundation were added numerous works brought from Italy after the French victories, but only a small number remained after the restitutions effected by the Allies in 1815. However, more Greek and Roman antiquities soon came to enrich the museum once more and incessant acquisitions, continuing up to our own days, have made of this department one of main world centres of classical archeology. Its collections fill the Mollien and Daru galleries, the Sphinx Courtyard and the ground floor of the South-West quarter of the buildings round the Square Courtyard; also the rooms on the first floor of the South wing of this courtyard, over-looking the Seine, as well as the Henri II Room and the Bronze Room in the West wing.

There is not a chapter in the history of the art of antiquity, from the origins of Hellenism (33) to the last days of the Roman Empire, which is not illustrated here either simultaneously or successively and often with great distinction, by marbles, bronzes, ceramics, gold and silver work, ivories, glasswork, frescos.

This brilliant review is illustrated by so many masterpieces of sculpture that it becomes difficult to make a choice. For the archaic period extending from the 7th century BC to the beginning of the 5th century AD, we must certainly mention two pieces: the Dorian *Lady of Auxerre* (34) and the Ionian *Hera of Samos* (35). A comparison shows clearly the difference between the two principal currents underlying Greek art. The first piece—so named because it formed part of a collection from the neighbourhood of Auxerre—is one of the earliest known examples of Greek statuary (second half of the 7th century BC). The small, solidly built body stands with feet together, sheathed in a

33. Cycladic idol, Amorgos, marble
(2nd half of the 3rd millenary)

34. Lady of Auxerre
(2nd half of 7th cen.BC)

35. Hera of Samos
(1st half 6th cen.BC)

36. Rampin head
(mid 6th cen.BC)

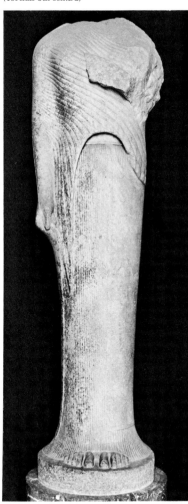

37. Hercules and the Cretan bull,
Olympia (ap.460 BC)

38. The "Ergastines", frieze of the Panathenean,
Parthenon (442-432 BC)

stiff tunic, bound at the waist by a wide bely, the
shoulders covered by a short cape. A heavy, Egyptian-
style wig covers the head. The sober severity of the
style shows that it initiated in Crete. The second is
more recent (first half of the 6th century) and the
cylindric form, revealing the influence of Mesopotania,
indicates a very different approach: the delicate
modelling of barely-indicated forms, the mysterious
life which seems to animate them, the lightness and
elegance of the draperies are characteristic of Ionia,
from whence it comes. This statue probably figures
the wife of Zeus. In any case it was dedicated to
this goddess by a certain Cheramyes, as we see by
the inscription it bears. We must also mention, among
all the pieces which bear witness in the Louvre
Museum to Greek archaism, the *Rampin head* (about
560 BC), that "masterpiece of intense delicacy and
decorative charm" (J. Charbonneaux). It formed part
of the statue of a victorious cavalier whose torso and
part of the body of his horse are in the Acropolis
Museum in Athens.

The classical period, and specially the 5th century,
is represented in our collections by numerous pieces
of high quality detached statuary, such as the famous
Laborde Head, where mingle gentleness, purity and
energy. This head has been recognised as that of the
Nika driving the chariot of Athena which decorates

39. Apollo slaving Lizards,
replica of an original
by Praxiteles (ap.350 BC)

40. Borghese Gladiator (1st cen.BC)

41. The Victory of Samothrace
(end 3rd- beginning 2nd cen.BC)

43. Bust of Agrippa
(beginning 1st cen.AD)

44. Portrait of Annius Verus
(ap.160 BC)

42. Venus of Milo
(end 2nd cen.BC)

45. Altar of Domitius Ahenobarbus
central part (end 2nd- beginning 1st cen.BC)

46. Frieze of the Ara Pacis, fragment
(end 1st cen.BC)

47. Apollo of the Piombino
(ap.500 BC)

inspired, like the whole decoration of the Parthenon, by Phidias—are no less characteristic of the Attic art which combines in a novel and harmonious manner the opposing qualities of Dorism and Ionism. This solemn procession of young girls who have woven the veil to be offered every four years to Athena, reveals an extreme care in its execution, a discreet skill in the rhythm, a majesty at once lively and graceful in the attitudes, which give an impression of true perfection.

48. Engraved Etruscan mirror
(4th cen.BC)

49. Goblet from Boscoreale
(ap. 1st cen.AD)

the West pediment of the Parthenon in Athens. Here again, however, it is through the juxtaposition of two essential works—reliefs in this case—that we can best understand both the definitive progess accomplished by Greek art in the course of one century and the artistic characteristics of each of the two main schools from which it grew. These are a metope from the temple of Zeus at Olympia, built between 470 and 460 BC, and a fragment of the Panathenians frieze from the Parthenon, executed, like the Laborde head, between 442 and 432 BC (37, 38). The strong, simple composition in intersecting diagonals of *Hercules subduing the Cretan bull*, the solid, robust forms of the bodies, the rather dry modelling which makes the muscles seen to stand out by accentuating the shadows, are typical of the Dorian technique. The *Ergastines—*

From the 4th century on, the Greek artists were increasingly attracted by humanistic truth and gradually abandoned the classical ideal. The pathetic quality of Scopas, the sensuality of Praxiletes, the heroic style of Lysippus opened the way for Hellenistic sculpture. Numerous works on exhibit in our galleries testify to this evolution. If we confine ourselves to masculine types, we find the *Apollo slaying Lizards* (39), the original of which was created by Praxiletes about 350 BC, or the *Borghese Gladiator* (40) signed by an artist of the 1st century BC, Agasias of Ephesius, who was obviously inspired by a Lysippic model.

Two statues of this period must be mentioned because of their contribution to the universal renown of the Louvre Museum: the *Victory of Samothrace* (41) and the *Venus of Milo* (42). The first, upright,

50. The Judgement of Paris, mosaic from Antioch
(ap.2nd cen.AD)

with spread wings at the prow of a galley, seems to resist the wind which flattens the supple draperies against the body. It probably commemorates a naval victory of the Rhodians at the end of the 3rd or beginning of the 2nd centuries BC. At Samothrace it must have been placed in a great niche towering above an "architectural landscape". It is supposed, since the discovery in 1950 of the open right hand, that the right arm of the figure was held hight to announce this victory. The original Aphrodite discovered in 1820 in the island of Milo is considered to be a masterpiece of antique art and, in general, as one of the most perfect examples of female beauty. Stylistic particularities give serious reasons to suppose it dates from the end of the second century BC: "the proportions of the body, the fluidity of line, the deliberate contrast between the elaborate folds of the draperies and the nudity of the body" (Charbonneaux), in spite of the serene expression on the face, which was thought at one time to suggest the genius of Praxiletes.

Finally, a large place in our collections is occupied by sculptures of the Roman period. All demonstrate in varying degree what the art of Rome and the provinces owed to that of Greece and the Hellenic world. However, the numerous portraits or historic reliefs represent two branches which show real originality. The abundant series of statues, busts and heads, effigies of emperors, members of the royal family or mere individuals, constitute a veritable history of portraiture, from the republican period to the Lower Empire. Certain of these pieces count among the masterpieces of the genre. Among them we note the bust of *Agrippa* (43), associate and son-in-law of Augustus, or the basalt head of *Livia*, wife of that Emperor, or again, the moving and exquisite one of *Annius Verus* (44), Marcus-Aurelius, young son, who died at the age of seven. In the same way, we can follow, from the end of the 2nd century BC to the 2nd century AD, the evolution of the historical reliefs which constituted the chief decoration on the Roman commemorative buildings. The oldest and certainly the most typical of these "sculpted pictures" in the Louvre, is the frieze which adorned one side of a great rectangular basis consecrated in Neptune's temple in Rome and to which has been given—erroneously, as it seems—the title of *Altar of Domitius Ahenobarbus* (the three other sides of this frieze are in the Glyptothecus in Munich). Essentially, it portrays the sacrifice of Suovetaurilia. On either side of the altar, in the central part (45) we see the god Mars and a magistrate, probably in the act of concecrating it. Beside it, a fragment of the frieze of the famous *Aras Pacis* (46), altar of Peace consecrated in Rome by Agustus in 9 BC, appears more Grecian, because of the quality of the line, the variety of attitudes and draperies and the type of relief. The procession it portrays is none the less Roman with its diversity of grounds, densely grouped figures and specially the realism of the scene, which is not idealised as it is in the procession of the Ergastines.

The bronzes too are just as important for an understanding of sculpture—specially in the case of a masterpiece like the *Apollo of Piombino* (47), probably

51. Idol-bell,
Beotia (ap.700 BC)

52. Proto Corinthean vase
in the form of an owl
(7th cen.BC)

53. Hercules and Antea,
chalice-shaped bowl for mixing wine,
atributed to Euphronios
(ap.510 BC)

from a Peloponnesian studio about 500 BC. Through them, we can discover numerous aspects of the Greek, Etruscan and Roman civilisations. In this room, statues, statuettes, small figures, adjoin quantities of other objects, chosen for their decoration or usage, or both at once: mirrors (48), cists, lamps, armour, furniture, various utensils. Greco-Roman gold and silver-work was less abundant but is represented in the Louvre by a magnificent collection of jewels in gold and by numerous pieces of silver, the most famous of which were discovered at *Boscoreale*, near Pompei (49).

Several fine examples of frescos and, indirectly, mosaics bear witness to the quality of Greco-Roman painting, but in this form of antique art, the museum is noted above all for its series of ceramics. Its world-famous collection of Greek vases, exhibited in the rooms of the Campana Gallery—named after the extremely rich collection bought in 1863—provides a complete panorama of all the schools and styles, from the so-called geometric ceramics (9th-8th centuries BC) to the most recent Hellenistic productions (2nd century BC) (51, 52, 53). Here we have historical documents, but also original works of art (whereas the great majority of Greek sculpture and painting is known only through copies dating from the Roman period). Some are signed by great masters, such as Exekias (about 550-530 BC)—Attic ceramic with figures in black –or Euphronios (520-500 BC)—Attic ceramic with figures in red. Then, in the last room of the same gallery, we find the best pieces of an important collection of small terra-cotta figures. The pieces executed in the studios of Tanagra (54) and Myrina, during the Hellenistic period are especially famous.

54. The "Sophoclean Woman", tanagra (end 4th cen.BC)

Paintings

The collection of paintings in the Louvre may not be the largest of any museum in the world, but it is doubtless the most complete. It origined in the "pictures cabinet", constituted at Fontainebleau by François I. This collection was greatly enriched by Louis XIV—an inventory drawn up in 1709-1710 mentions nearly fifteen hundred paintings—then further increased, after the fall of the Monarchy, by property confiscated from the Church and the émigrés, then, after the revolutionary and imperial conquests, by plunder from various European countries. It was considerably reduced by the restitutions made in 1815 but took on new life, specially from the Second Empire on. Since then, there have been numerous donations and pur-

chases, with the department following a policy of eclectic acquisitions in conformity with the diversity of its stock. It occupies nearly all the first floor of the part of the palace situated to the West of Apollo's Gallery—notably in the Square Room, the Great Gallery and the Estates' Room—as well as the second floors of the West and South wings on the side of the Square Courtyard.

It is not surprising that two-thirds of the paintings in the Louvre should belong to the French School. First come the main pieces of the 14th and 15th centuries, such as the *Pietà of Villeneuve-lès-Avignon* (57), an austere and grandiose masterpiece from the late Middle Ages, now attributed to Enguerrand

55. Anonymous
Portrait of King Jean-le-Bon (ap.1360)

56. Jean Fouquet
Portrait of King Charles VII (ap.1445)

57. Enguerrand Quentin
Pietà of Villeneuve-lès-Avignon (ap.1460)

58. Fontainebleau School
Diana Huntress (ap.1550)

59. Antoine Caron
Massacre of the Triumvirs, central section (1566)

Quarton, a native of the diocese of Laon, but who is known to have worked in Provence from 1444 to 1446; or the anonymous portrait of King *Jean le Bon* (55) executed about 1360. This is the oldest known French easel-painting, as well as the first of a kind for which Jean Fouquet, notably, became known during the next century, specially with a *Charles VII* (56) where the compact lay-out is still remniscent of the Gothic style. This type of painting, in which Clouet excelled, was still flowering during the 16th century when the Italian decorators brought to Fontainebleau by François I, introduced into France a Manierist art, all elegance and subtilty, such as we see in this *Diana Huntress* (58) by an unknown master (about 1550) which is thought to have been an idealised portrait of King Henri II's favourite, Diane de Poitiers. Few of the painters influenced by the Fontainebleau School had such a powerful personality as Antoine Caron.

His *Massacre of the Triumvirs*, dated 1566, is strongly allegorical, in the fashion of the day, and constitutes a barely veiled allusion to the first horrors of the Wars of Religion.

At the beginning of the 17th century, after a first period of crisis, the French artists sought to revive their art directly in Italy, and specially in Rome. Most of them, like Valentin or Vignon, discovered what they sought in the works of Caravaggio, with his religious themes or scenes of life among the ordinary people, and his dramatic, strongly contrasted lighting. Georges de la Tour too was influenced by this powerful renovator of European painting. He shows a fondness for homelike, night-time scenes with an atmosphere of mystery (60) produced by the flickering light of a torch or candle, but also by the very personal simplification of forms and the soberly harmonious colours which are equally original. The three Le Nain

60. Georges de La Tour
St. Joseph Carpenter (ap.1640)

61. Louis Le Nain
Peasant Family (ap.1643)

62. Nicolas Poussin
Shepherds of Arcadia (ap.1640)

63. Claude Gelée, known as Le Lorrain
Sea-port (1639)

64. Philippe de Champagne
Ex-voto 1662

65. Antoine Watteau
Gilles (ap.1718)

66. Hyacinthe Rigaud
Louis XIV in Coronation Robes (1701)

67. Honoré Fragonard
Women Bathing (ap.1770)

68. Jean-Baptiste Greuze. The Broken Pitcher (1777)

69. Louis David. Oath of the Horacios (1784)

70. Antoine Gros. Bonaparte visiting victims
of the Plague at Jaffa (right section) (1804)

71. Pierre-Paul Prod'hon
The Empress Josephine (1805)

72. Louis David
Coronation of Napoleon I at Notre-Dame in Paris, on December 2nd 1804 (1805-1807)

73. Théodore Géricault
The Raft of the *Méduse* (1819)

74. Eugène Delacroix
Liberty guiding the People (1830)

brothers were even more attracted by the realities of everyday life. It was certainly Louis, with his sensibility entirely free of affectation, who best expressed the rusticity as well as the dignity of these humble lives.

Nicolas Poussin, supreme master of French classicism, theorist, philosopher and poet, spent nearly all his life in Rome. More than any other artist of his time, he was obsessed by the desire for perfection. The landscapes in which he enframed his biblical, mythological or historical subjects, finally became his main theme (62) Claude Gellée too—known as Le Lorrain— was a "Roman" and a landscape-painter, but less intellectual, more anecdotal, more lyrical. He was interested above all in the study of light, with its variations at different times of day and its reflection in water, and he is sometimes considered as one of the precursors of Impressionism.

Portrait-painting was not neglected by our 17th century painters and it gave a number of rich temperaments the chance to express themselves fully. Philippe de Champagne was of Flemish origin and official painter to Louis XIII and Richelieu, then the recognised iconographer of Jansenism. Thus his greatest masterpiece, *Ex-voto 1662* (64) executed in gratitude to God for the recovery of his daughter Catherine, a nun at Port-Royal, portrays her beside Mother Agnès Arnauld at the moment when the miracle is revealed to the Abbess. This austere, fervent act of thanksgiving has little in common with the sprightly, academic manner of Charles Le Brun's *Chancellor Séguier* (about 1655-1657) or Hyathinthe Rigaud's solemn and sumptuous *Louis XIV* (1701) (66), but they too are admired for the subtle psychological observation of the faces in both of these compositions.

75. Eugène Delacroix
Portrait of Frédéric Chopin (1838)

76. Théodore Chassériau
Esther at her Toilet (1842)

77. Jean-Dominique Ingres
The Turkish Bath (1862)

78. Camille Corot
Recollection of Mortefontaine (1862)

79. Jean-François Millet
The Gleaners (1857)

80. Gustave Courbet
The Painter's Studio (central section)
(1855)

At the dawn of the 18th century, the novelty of Antoine Watteau's subjects and techniques opened up new possibilities in painting. He was often inspired by scenes and characters from the contemporary theatre in France and Italy and his portrait of a comedian, *Gilles* (65), is at once symbolic and personal. It is considered by some to be a self-portrait. This delicate colorist and no less remarkable draughtsman gave full play to his genius by transposing these subjects into a world of dream or fairy. As the painter of "Gay Parties", he was received into the Royal Academy of Painting and Sculpture on August 28th 1717, where he presented the *Embarkation for Cytherus*, a second version of which is conserved in the Charlottenburg Palace in Berlin. This sensitive, poetic art set the fashion for several decades of French painting, We find it in the elegant genre of François Boucher, though his art was more licencious and decorative; in that of Henri Fragonard (67)—more intimist and executed with greater brio—and in the still-lives and portraits (113) of Jean-Baptiste Chardin which rejoin the realistic trend. Even the moralistic Jean-Baptiste Greuze was fashionably graceful in *The Broken Pitcher* (1777) (68).

During the second half of the 18th century, there was an increasingly strong reaction against a style of painting which began to seem too witty, too charming, too much preoccupied with everyday things. Archeological discoveries renewed the admiration for Greco-Roman antiquity, while at the same time there grew up a deep and generalised idealism which demanded a simpler, more serious and more heroic type of art. This aspiration gave birth to the Neo-classical movement, of which the *Oath of the Horacios* (69), the great success of the 1785 Salon, was a sort of manifesto. In the work of Louis David we find all the elements of Neo-classicism: the moral or historical grandure of his subjects, a composition with the rythmic balance of an antique bas-relief, noble attitudes, anatomical precision, and primary importance accorded to drawing rather than to colour... The Revolution, then the Napoleonic epic, gave this imperious doctrinairian and his pupils a chance to give brilliant expression to their ideas. David could show all his talent for portrait-painting in *The Coronation* (72), painted between 1805 and 1807, while *Bonaparte visiting victims of the Plague at Jaffa* (70), executed in the space of a few

months by Antoine Gros, is one of the largest and most famous canvases in the Louvre. In spite of official blessing, however, Neo-Classicism did not reign unchallenged. The sensibility and poetic charm of Pierre-Paul Prud'hon (71) prolonged the graceful manner of the 18th century, while hints of Romanticism are already evident in the work of Anne-Louis Girodet. Perhaps, indeed, we can detect something of the same presentiment in the colour and epic inspiration of *Victims of the Plague at Jaffa*.

The *Raft of the Meduse* (73), presented at the 1819 Salon by Théodore Géricault, is often considered to be the first manifestation of French Romanticism in painting. This illustration of a contemporary incident (the survival of fifteen people shipwrecked after the loss of a frigate that had set out for Senegal in July 1816) is executed with a passion and dramatic force which give it a place among the great masterpieces of French painting and justify, in any case, its exhibition in the same gallery as the works of Eugène Delacroix, which mark the triumph of the new shool. Triumph of colour, movement, emotion... Here is a revolution and we may wonder which of the sixty odd canvases of brilliant painter best represent it? The revolutionary *Freedom guiding the People* (74) inspired by the events of July 1830? Or one may prefer the more sober Delacroix of *The Taking of Constantinople by the Crusaders* (1841) in which the tumultuous movement of the preceding work is moderated and harmonised by the nobility of the composition. We should be neglecting an essential aspect of this sumptuous colorist if we did not mention the *Women of Algiers in their Apartment* (1834) in which light plays such an important part; nor could we understand this tormented nature if we forget the *Portrait of Frédéric Chopin* (1838) (75) in which we see all the anguish of romantic creation.

It is traditional to compare Eugène Delacroix with Jean-Dominique Ingres: the magician of colourful masses with the poet of forms; the admirer of the Venetians and of Rubens with that of the 15th century Florentines and of Raphael, dedicated to the pure lines and subtle curves also learned from the paintings on Greek vases; the ardent defender of the imagination with the clear, realistic mind, with its classical distinctness and honest observation. Three paintings typify, each in its own way, the aesthetics of this calm, solid bourgeois, who was yet inspired in the most voluptuous way by his devotion for the beauty of the female form. The *Apotheosis of Homer* (1827) is a composition destined to decorate a ceiling of the Louvre, where it was to constitute a sort of profession of faith; the *Portrait of M. Bertin* (1832), founder of the «Journal des Débats», is an almost symbolic representation of the upper-middle class of the day; the *Turkish Bath* (1862) (77) is the synthesis and outcome of a long life dedicated to research on the theme of Bathing Women. An "Ingrist" school grew up in its turn. Théodore Chassériau was able to conciliate successfully the art of his master with that of his rival: his *Esther at her Toilet* (1842) (76) is a worthy successor to both of them.

Romanticism reawoke a taste for Nature, which plays an important part in French painting from 1830 on. The Louvre possesses over a hundred and thirty canvases of Camille Corot, who illustrates this trend. Though he followed the clasical tradition handed down by Poussin and Claude Lorrain, the poetic freshness of his approach and an increasingly evident interest in the subtle play of light resulted in a freedom of plastic expression which reveals him as a forerunner of Impressionism (78). Most of the other landscape-painters followed in the footsteps of the Dutch painters of the 17th century; several of them settled on the edge of the Forest of Fontainebleau, at Barbizon, which gave its name to a school. The most illustrious was Jean-François Millet, who revealed the dignity inherent in the hard peasant-life through the nobility of the scenes where he shows them at work in the fields (79).

This concern with social problems is emphasised by the powerful brushwork of Honoré Daumier in several of his paintings. With Gustave Courbet, it took on a Socialist aspect. *The Artist's studio* (1855) (80) is a "true allegory", which expresses in a masterly composition his conception of "living art". Here the leader of the Naturalist school shows himself at work on a landscape of his native Franche-Comté, surrounded by his Muse, Truth, and his friends (Baudelaire, Champfleury, Proud'hon) on the right, and, on the left, representatives of various classes of society—"exploiters" together with the "exploited".

81. The Sermon to the Birds, from the predella of the altar-piece of St. Francis of Assisi (ap.1300)

Of all the foreign schools, the Italian is best represented in the Louvre, partly because it constituted the first, sumptuous royal collections of paintings, and also because it has always been highly appreciated in France. Each phrase of its evolution, from the second half of the 13th century to the end of the 18th, is illustrated here by several world-famous masterpieces.

Two vast panels, both from the Church of San Francesco in Pisa, bear brilliant witness to the early days of Florentine art: the majestic *Virgin and Angels* (about 1270) (82) by Cimabua, where we see the beginnings of a reaction against the hieratism of Byzance in the freer and more human attitudes of the figures; and *Saint Francis of Assisi receiving the Stigmata* (about 1300) (81) in which Giotto has achieved complete liberation. The *Carrying of the Cross*, executed by Simone Martini during his stay at the Papal Court in Avignon (1340-1344) is one wing-panel of a small portable polyptych, the other elements of which are

82. Cimabue
Virgin with Angels (ap.1270)

83. Andrea Mantegna
Calvary (1459)

84. Leonardo da Vinci
The Child and Saint Anne the Virgin,
(ap. 1506-1510)

in the Amsterdam Rijksmuseum and the Berlin-Dahlem Museum. Here, among the Primitives of other schools of the Peninsular, we see an example of the important contribution made by the artists of Sienna.

During the *Quattrocento* (15th century) Italian painting began to evolve, under the dual influence of architecture and sculpture, in the direction of the Renaissance. Though the *Coronation of the Virgin* (85) executed by Fra Angelico in 1434-1435 for the Church of San Domenico in Fiesole, is still Mediaeval in its choice of subject and mystic treatment, it reveals a new orientation in our collections: the scope and balance of the structure, the respect for perspective, the arrangement of the figures, freed from the traditional organisation, are obvious signs of a modernism which becomes even more evident in the scenes from the life of Saint Dominic shown in the predella. Paolo Ucello too was an inovator when he painted in 1455 for the Medicis, the episode from the *Battle of San Romano* (86) in the possession of the Louvre—a second is in the Uffizi Galleries in Florence, and a third in the National Gallery in London. The care with which depth and volume are rendered by bold foreshortening, the decorative stylisation of the forms, emphasised by the warm colouring, give to this work the monumental appearance of a haut-relief. The *Calvary* (83) with which Andrea Mantegna decorated the central part of the predella of an altar-piece for the church of San Zeno in Verona—the lateral parts are in the museum of Tours—is more chiselled, more geometrical, more skilful. Two large compositions by Sandro Botticelli show him torn between Christianism and humanism. Here, we find the sharp, sinuous brushwork, delicate, transparent colouring, and extreme refinement of style that so well express the mannered grace of allegorical figures with their melancholy, mysterious countenances, such as we see in the frescos (88) datable 1483, from the Villa Lemmi (near Florence) originally the property of the Tornabuonis, friends of the Medicis.

The "golden age" (end of the 15th to middle of the 16th centuries) of the Italian Renaissance is brilliantly illustrated in the Louvre. First, we have an ensemble, such as can be found nowhere else in the world, of works by Leonardo da Vinci, beginning with the most universally admired and discussed of

85. Fra Angelico
Coronation of the Virgin (1434-1435)

86. Paolo Ucello
The Battle of San Romano (ap.1450-1455)

87. Raphael
The Holy Family, known as
La Belle Jardinière (1507)

88. Sandro Botticelli
Fresco from the Villa Lemmi (ap.1483)

89. Titien
Deposition (ap.1525)

paintings: the portrait which may reasonably be supposed to represent Monna Lisa Gherardini, married in 1495 to the Florentine patrician Francesco del Giocondo and which is thus known as the Monna Lisa (p. 2). Da Vinci was so fond of this painting that he took it with him when François I invited him to France in 1516 and he settled near Ambroise, in the château de Cloux, where he died three years later. The Monna Lisa then became the most precious piece in the King's "Cabinet of Paintings". Everything has been said about the enigmatic smile, the marvellous modelling of the face, the way the tone values shade off so that the light seems to slide over the forms, the vapourous, dreamlike atmosphere of the landscape in the background. In the same way, the mysterious poetry and already perfect skill of the *Virgin of the*

Rocks, ordered in 1483 by the Fraternity of the Conception of San Francesco Grande in Milan, has been the subject of continual study. The same is true of the symbolism and spirituality of *The Child, the Virgin and Saint Anne* (64), a work executed several years after the Monna Lisa and ordered by the Servites of Florence for the high altar of their church.

Several paintings by Raphael now in the Louvre once belonged to François I. This was probably the case of the *Virgin and Child with St John the Baptist* (87), signed and dated 1507, and the finest example in our collections of the perfect harmony to which this artist aspired. Raphael's portrait, painted about 1514-1515, of his friend *Balthazar Castiglione*, poet, diplomat, "the finest knight in all the world", according to the Emperor Charles-Quint. Louis XIV

90. Veronese
Mariage Feast of Cana,
detail (1563)

91. Francesco Guardi
The Doge on his way to the Salute (ap.1770)

acquired it from Mazarin's heirs in 1661. In the same year and from the same source, Correggio's *Antiope asleep* (about 1524-1525), was acquired for the royal collections. This work was well-known in its day and is less intellectual, more relaxed and sensual than the former.

This tendency triumphed magnificently in Venice, wher until the end of the 16th century, the Venetian artists painted, not out of piety nor to try their skill, but simply to give direct expression to their feelings about landscape, draperies, or the nude body. They preferred masses of light and colour to the refined line and delicate modelling dear to the Florentines. Giorgione was to be the innovator of this "maniera moderna" and his pupil Titian its most illustrious

92. Caravaggio
Death of the Virgin (ap.1605)

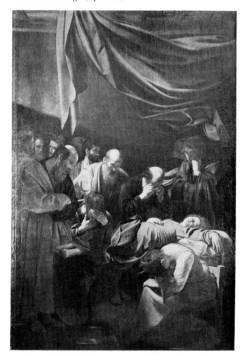

representative. Is the *Rustic Concert* the work of the master or his disciple? It is dated 1510-1511 and was attributed for a long time to Giorgione but nowadays it is more often considered to be by Titian. In any case, a stylistic comparison shows a close resemblance with the latter's *Entombment* (89), executed about fifteen years later and added to the royal collections, together with the *Rustic Concert* in 1671. The Louvre possesses two outstanding examples of the decorative style splendidly developed by the Venetian painters of the following generation: the gigantic *Marriage Feast of Cana* (90) by Veronese, which was ordered in 1562 and finished in 1563 for the refectory of the convent of San Giorgio Maggiore in Venice, and the reduced-size sketch for the huge composition, *Paradise*, ordered from Tintoretto in 1588 to decorate the Great Council Hall of the Serenissime, in the Palace of the Doges.

Towards the end of the 16th century, a new kind of art began to develop in Italy. In 1585, the Carracho brothers founded in Bologna an Academy—the first School of Art—where they taught an eclectic approach, which tends towards naturalism in the landscapes of Annibal Carrachio, such as the *Hunting* and *Fishing* in the Louvre. Caravaggio is more revolutionary, and his aesthetics and technique were to have a strong influence on European painting, specially in France. His *Death of the Virgin* (92) ordered in 1605 for the church of Santa Maria in Trastevere in Rome, created a scandal because of a realism considered too plebian and accentuated by the contrast between the zones of light and shade that was judged too dramatic. It was admired nevertheless by those who recognised in it the signs of a coming regeneration.

Eighteenth century Venice saw the last great days of Italian painting. The most noteworthy works of this period in our collections are those of Francesco Guardi, with a series of canvases—eight out of the original twelve—commemorating the festivities organised for the coronation of the Doge Alvo Mocenigo IV (91).

The Flemish and Dutch schools are less abundantly represented in the Louvre than the Italians, but we have numerous masterpieces sufficiently important to give an almost complete panorama of each.

For the earliest Flemish painters, we have two pieces of capital importance: Jan van Eyk's *Virgin of Autun* (about 1435) (93) which comes from the collegial

93. Jan van Eyck
The Virgin of Autun (ap.1435)

94. Hans Memling
Portrait of an Old Woman (ap.1470-1475)

95. Quentin Metsys
The Moneylender and his wife (1514)

96. Pieter Breughel the Elder
The Beggars (1568)

church of that city, to which it was donated by Nicolas Rolin, chancellor of Bourgogne; and Rogier van der Weyden's *Braque Triptych* (about 1452), probably executed for Catherine of Brabant, in memory of her deceased husband, Jehan Braque. Among the works of the second half of the 15th century, several paintings by Hans Memling attract attention, specially his *Portrait of an Old Woman* (about 1470-1475) (94). Among those of the 16th century, we find *The Moneylender and his Wife* (1514) (95) by Quentin Metsys—one of the works at the origin of genre painting in the Netherlands; and Peter Breugel the Elder's *Beggars* (1568) (96), which has been interpreted as an allusion to the "Beggars' Revolt" against the government of Philip II of Spain. Peter-Paulus Rubens' supremacy in the Flemish school of the 17th century is brilliantly illustrated by the admirable portrait of his second wife, Helena Fourment and his children (about 1636); by the *Village Fair* (about 1635-1638), with its teeming

97. Pieter-Paulus Reubens
Marie de Medicis landing at Marseilles (1622-1625)

life, that several French artists (Watteau, Fragonard, Delacroix...) studied to their advantage; and above all, by the huge decorative ensemble executed between 1622 and 1625 at the request and in honour of Queen Marie de Medicis, for a gallery in the Luxembourg Palace. One of the best-known parts—and another source of inspiration for the same French artists—is the *Marie de Medicis landing at Marseilles* (97). Anton van Dyck, "Painter in Ordinary to the King", executed numerous portraits of *Charles I* of England. That in the Louvre (98) is considered as the finest. The *Four Evangelists* too (though it may represent *Christ explaining the Scriptures to the Doctors*) is one of the finest examples of the first period of Jacob Jordaens.

All the great names are excellently represented in the Dutch Collection. Jerome Bosch's great panel painting, *The Ship of Lunatics* (99), painted during the last years of the 15th century, is an almost surrealist allegory, stigmatising "follies" of taste and hearing, or more generally, the vices of his time. Lucas de Leyde's fantastic landscape, *Lot and his Daughters* (about 1509-1517) is a forerunner in Manierist style of the Dutch "luminisms" of the following century. From Franz Hals we have a so-called "character-portrait", *The Gypsy Girl* (about 1628) (101), remniscent of Caravaggio in its freedom and audacity. The delicate perfection of light, colour and brushwork in Jan Vermeer of Delft's *Lacemaker* (1664) (102) admirably expresses the serenity of domestic life by revealing its innate poetry, and Jacob van Ruysdael's *Sun-burst* (about 1670 is one of the finest landscape paintings in the world. The pride of our collection, however, is above all the impressive series of Rembrandts: portraits —specially self-portraits— like this supremely moving one (100) in which the artist shows himself at the age of fifty-four (1660), worn by sorrow, ruin and solitude, yet still confident in his art; biblical scenes, including the famous *Pilgrims at Emmaüs* (1648), in which the magical clair-obscur and extreme simplicity of composition combine to render the divine presence visible with an intensity seldom achieved by any painter; and a *Bethsabea* (1654) (103) at her toilet, holding in her hand the letter in which David declares his love. This is one of Rembrandt's rare nudes, for which he used his devoted second wife, Hendrickje Stoffels, as his model.

98. Anton van Dyck
Portrait of Charles 1st of England (ap.1635)

Our collection of German paintings is more modest, but we have several important pieces from the most glorious period of this school (end of 15th century) and notably: *Deposition* which formed the central part of a great tryptich executed about 1500 by the artist known as the Master of St. Bartholomew from the title of an altarpiece now in the Munich picture-gallery; a *Self-portrait* (104), painted by Albert Dürer when he was twenty-two (1493) supposedly for his fiancée (he holds in his hand a sort of thistle, symbol of fidelity); a charming *Venus* (1529) from the studio of Lucas Cranach the Elder; Hans Holbein the Younger's most famous portrait, that of *Erasmus*, the prince of humanism (1523) writing his "Commentary on the Gospel of St. Mark".

In the same way, though the English school has only a small place in the Louvre, it is brilliantly illustrated. For the 17th century we have portraits by Sir

99. Jerome Bosch
The Ship of Lunatics (ap.1490-1500)

100. Rembrandt
Portrait of the Painter in his Old Age (1660)

101. Frans Hals
The Gypsy Girl (1628-1630)

102. Jan Vermeer of Delft
The Lacemaker (1664)

103. Rembrandt
Bethsabia (1654)

104. Albrecht Dürer
Portrait of the Artist (1493)

Joshua Reynolds (105), founder of the Royal Academy, by his rival Thomas Gainsborough and by Sir Thomas Lawrence, painter to all the European courts. For the 19th century there are the romantic landscapes of John Constable, Richard Parkes Bonington and Joseph M.W. Turner. A canvas specially popular in the United States, *The Artist's Mother* (1872), by James M. Whistler must be counted among this collection of Anglo-Saxon paintings.

The Spanish collection is certainly less magnificent than that which was the personal property of Louis-Philippe and which, after having been exhibited in the Louvre from 1838 to 1848, followed the King in his exile to London, where it was dispersed at a public sale in 1853. Today, it is still notable for a fine series of masterpieces: primitives such as Martorell's Martyrdom of St. George (about 1430-1435); a *Christ on the Cross* (about 1580) (106), extremely typical of Greco; and especially fine examples of the "Golden Century" (17th century) such as Ribera's *Club-footed Man* (1642); Zurburan's *Funeral of St. Bonaventura* (about 1630); Murillo's *Young Beggar* (1650); Velazquez portrait of the *Infanta Margharita*, daughter of Philip IV (about 1655) (108); or Carreno de Miranda's *Mass for the Founding of the Order of the Trinitarians* (1666). Finally, there are several portraits by Goya, among them the splendid Marquesa de la Solana (about 1791-1794) (109).

105. Joshua Reynolds
Master Hare (1788-1789)

106. Greco
Crucifixion (ap.1580)

107. Hans Holbein the Younger
Portrait of Erasmus (1523)

108. Velasquez
Portrait of the Infanta Margharita (ap.1655)

109. Goya
Portrait of the Marquesa de la Solana
(ap.1791-1794)

Cabinet of Drawings

This cabinet is installed in the Flore wing and only a small part—pastels for the most part— of its exceptionally rich and varied stock in on permanent exhibition. The rest is carefully preserved from the light and climatic variations and is accessible for research on authorisation from the Curator's Office. Temporary exhibitions on a given theme are regularly organised however and are open to the public in a room opening out of the Cabinet at the same days and times as the museum.

110. Rembrandt
View of the Canal at Amersfoort, pen and brown wash (ap.1655)

111. Leonardo da Vinci
Isabelle d'Este, black chalk, red chalk and pastel (ap.1490)

112. Jean Dominique Ingres
The Stamaty Family, black lead pencil (1818)

113. Jean-Baptiste Chardin
Self-portrait, known as "in green lamp-shade", pastel (1775)

Sculptures

This department came into being when the Museum of French Monuments was suppressed in 1817, under the Restoration. Part of its collection was then moved, from the convent of Minor Augustinians to the Palace of the Louvre and has been continually enriched so that it now constitutes as complete a history as possible of French sculpture, from its origins to the end of the 19th century. It is arranged in chronological order on the ground floor of the building running parallel with the Seine, from the entrance to the Carroussel to the Flore Pavilion, as well as on the ground floor of the latter.

First come the Roman sculptures, mostly executed strictly in function of the fragments of architecture they decorate. One example is *Daniel in the Lions' Den* (114) from the end of the 11th century, on a recut capital from the church of Ste Geneviève in Paris. This was evidently inspired by the Orient, from a model

116. Virgin of Auvergne
(2nd half 12th cen.)

114. Daniel in the Lions' Den,
Paris (end 9th cen.)

115. Christ of Lavaudieu
(2nd quarter 12th cen.)

117. The Queen of Sheba,
Corbeil
(ap.1180-1190)

118. Charles V,
Paris
(ap.1390)

taken from some Sassanide material. Another is the
Prophet, leaning against a column from the cloister
of Notre-Dame-des-Doms in Avignon, from the second
half of the 12th century, in which we detect the
influence of the art of the Royal Gateway in Chartres.
The style of these works is rough, but their purity
and candour give added intensity to the expression,
as we see in the suffering *Head of Christ* (115) in
painted and gilded wood, from the first half of the
12th century, originating from Lavaudieu in the Haute
Loire, or in the grave, rustic *Virgin of Auvergne* (116),
instrument of the Incarnation and the Word, from the
next half of the century.

119. Virgin and Child,
La Celle (1st quarter 14th cen.)

120. Antoine le Moiturier
Tomb of Philippe Pot (last quarter 15th cen.)

121. Jean Goujon
Bas-relief on the Fountain of the Holy Innocents (1547-1549)

122. Germain Pilon
The Three Graces
(ap.1560)

123. Simon Guillain
Anne of Austria
(1643)

124. Michel Colombe
St. George in Combat with the Dragon (early 16th cen.)

The statue-columns, *Solomon* and above all the *Queen of Sheba* (about 1180-1190) (117), from the old church of Notre-Dame at Corbeil are the last reflections of the great art of Rome and herald the coming of a more brilliant, supple and attractive Gothic art. This is represented in the Louvre by a series of masterpieces sufficiently complete to allow us to follow its evolution from the beginning to the end: pieces from the chief stoneyards of the 13th century, such as the Sainte Geneviève which decorated the pier-glass of the old Paris church of which she was the patron, or the fragment of the choir-screen from the cathedral of Chartres showing *Saint Mathew the Evangelist* writing at the dictation of an angel; Virgins with Child of the 14th century, among which the statue from the church of La Celle (Seine-et-Marne) (119) stands out for the high quality of the workmanship and counts among the finest treasures of our Mediaeval collections; recumbant or standing effigies of sovereigns, such as the St Louis in the likeness of Charles V (118), executed about 1390 for the doorway of the "Hospice des Quinze-Vingts", in which we already see the realism which was to be carried almost to caricatural lengths at the beginning of the next century, but which is tempered here with subtle indulgence. An example of the new tendency towards caricature is to be seen in the *Head of an Apostle* from the church of Mehun-sur-Yèvre (Cher), attributed to Jean de Cambrai. This brilliant panorama ends with the presentation of French and Burgundian sculptures cf the 15th century, grouped around one of the most famous masterpieces in our museum: the *Tomb of Philippe Pot* (120), Grand Senes-was carved by Antoine le Moiturier between 1477 and 1483 for the abbey church of Citeaux.
and 1483 for the abbey church of Citeaux.

During the 16th century, French sculpture was under the influence of the Italian Renaissance and became more delicate, more subtle, less naive. At the same time, it grew more ornamental, utilising decorative elements from the Transalpine repertory. Perhaps the monument which best represents its complex evolution during the first decades is the altarpiece of *St. George* (124), executed in Tours for the upper chapel of the château de Gaillon by Michel Colombe, one of the last Gothic "carvers" with a framework in the new style, carved for it on the spot by an Italian

125. Pierre Puget
Milon of Croton (1682)

126. Jean-Antoine Houdon
Portrait of Buffon (1783)

workshop. The triumph of the classical Renaissance during the second half of the century is illustrated by a series of outstanding pieces, such as Jean Goujon's bas-reliefs for the *Fountain of the Holy Innocents* (1547-1549) decorated with nymphs and tritons of indiscutably pagan sensuality (121); Pierre Bontemps funeral statue of *Admiral Philippe Chabot* (about 1570) showing him lying in an attitude revived from Etruscan statuary; Germain Pilon's *Three Graces* (122) for the monument containing the heart of Henri II (between 1560-1566), inspired by a famous antique group; or the same artist's statue of *Cardinal de Birague* at prayer (1584-1585) in which the decorative fullness of the folds of the great robe herald the more mobile art of the following century.

During the 17th and 18th centuries, French sculpture was marked by various successive or contrasting tendencies—classicism, realism, manierism, baroque—and it too is plentifully represented in the Louvre. Here we have triumphal monuments like that raised in 1643 on the "Pâté du Pont-au-Changes", which grouped the bronze effigies of Louis XIII, the Dauphin and Queen *Anne of Austria* (123) by Simon Guillan; funeral monuments such as the elegant obelisk raised about 1663 by François Anguier in the Chapel of the Celestins in Paris to commemorate the *Ducs de Longueville*; statues designed to ornament parks, like Puget's

127. François Rude
The Marseillaise, study (1834)

128. Antoine Coysevox
The Seine (1706)

129. Jean-Baptiste Pigalle
Mercury (1744)

130. Antoine-Louis Barye
Tiger springing on a Stag (1833)

spirited *Milon de Croton* (1682) (125) for Versailles, or the powerful statue of the *Seine* (1706) (128) by Coysevox, for Marly; pieces for reception at the Academy, such as Pigalle's graceful *Mercury binding on his sandal* (1744) (129) or Falconnet's no less famous *Woman bathing* (1755); and portraits, the long series of which ends with the rich and varied work of Houdon (126).

The Venetian Canova (126) set the example for the neo-classicsm of the revolutionary and imperial periods, then, from 1830 on, sculpture began to tend towards romanticism. Rude (127) was the most vigourous representative of this trend, which is also evident in the bronzes of Barye, with his accurate studies of animal life (130). This splendid review of French sculpture concludes with works by Carpeaux which are

131. Antonio Canova
Psyche and Cupid (1793)

132. Jean-Baptiste Carpeaux
Dance (1869)

sometimes joyful and sometimes tormented, but always full of vitality. His group entitled "The Dance" (132), has recently been replaced by a copy on the façade of the Opera Theatre.

For the 15th and 16th centuries principally, we present for comparison pieces from the schools of neighbouring States: the Netherlands, Germany, Spain and especially Italy. Among them are two world-famous masterpieces: those known as the *Dying Slave* (133) and the *Rebel Slave* by Michelangelo, sculpted between 1513-1515 for the tomb of Pope Julius II. They were finally discarded from the monument and presented by the artist to his friend Roberto Strozzi, who offered them in hommage to King Henri II of France, who presented them in his turn to the High Constable de Montmorency. They remained in the latter's home at Ecouen until they passed in 1632 to Cardinal de Richelieu, who placed them in his chateau in Poitou, from whence the Marechal de Richelieu had them moved to his Paris mansion in 1749. In 1792 they passed to the Museum of French Monuments and from there to the Louvre in 1794. They were generally considered to be allegories of the liberal arts reduced to impotence by the death of their patron the Pope, but nowadays it seems more likely that, like the images of captives on the antique triumphal arches, they were conceived to symbolise on the lower part of the monument "the terrestial counterpart of the apotheosis of the Sovereign Pontiff portrayed at the summit". In any case, their imposing, tortured beauty gives intense expression, in a new manner and although—or perhaps because—they are unfinished, to Michelangelo's personal anguish at the time when he was at the height of his genius.

133. Michelangelo
The Dying Slave (1513-1515)

Objets d'Art

The precious objects and furniture in a section separated from the sculpture rooms since 1893, are exceptionaly valuable, both from the historical and the artistic point of view. They come from the royal collections, from property confiscated during the Revolution, from the transfer to the Louvre in 1901 of the old National Museum of Furniture and from numerous donations and purchases up to our own times. They are exhibited above the Small Gallery, in the Apollo Gallery, so-called because the painter Lebrun, who was entrusted with its decoration by Louis XIV in 1661, took as his theme the Sun-God, emblem of the sovereign. Eugène Delacroix adopted the same theme in 1848, when the gallery was renovated by Duban and he painted the central part with *Apollo vanquishing the Serpent Python.*

The objects shown in the Apollo Gallery are a great attraction both for their precious material and for the manner in which they illustrate the glories of the history of France. Some formed part of the Crown Jewels, like the famous 137 carat "Regent diamond", acquired in 1717 by Philippe d'Orléans, Regent during the minority of Louis XV, or the crown worn by that sovereign at his coronation (135); others were part of the ornaments or "regalia" of coronation, such as the golden sceptre surmounted by a statue of Charlemagne (134), chiselled for Charles V in the 14th century; or of the treasure of the royal Abbey of St. Denis, or of the Order of the Holy Ghost, founded in 1578 by Henri III. Certain pieces in these ensembles, however, are above all works of art: the *porphery vase* (136) in the form of a hierarchical eagle (silver-gilt) ordered by Suger, abbott of St. Denis in the 12th century; or the silver-gilt *Virgin*, known as that of *Jeanne d'Evreux* (137) presented to the Abbey by that Queen in 1339; or the parade shield, plated with gold and enamel, executed for Charles IX (1550-1574).

134. Sceptre of Charles V
(last quarter 14th cen.)

135. Eagle Vase, known as Suger vase
(mid 12th cen.)

136. Crown from the coronation
of Louis XV (1722)

137. Virgin of Jeanne d´Evreux
silver-gilt, Paris (1339)

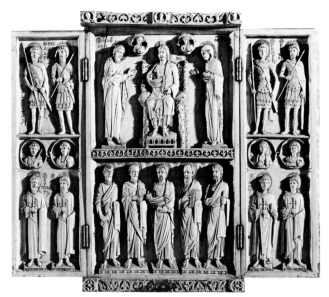

138. Harbaville Triptych
Byzantium (?) (mid 15th cen.)

139. Coronation of the Virgin
ivory polychrome (3rd quarter 13th cen.)

140. Shoulder-plate,
known as that of the Resurrection,
copper-gilt and enamel,
Meuse (ap.1175-1180)

The old "Council Chamber" of the Château Neuf at Vincennes and the "King's Chamber" and "King's State Chamber" of the Louvre, (on the site of the present Seven Chimneys Room) have been partly reconstituted with the original panelling in the Colonnade Rooms. Here are exhibited an abundant and varied series of objects which are equally important for the history of the art the Middle Ages and the Renaissance: Paleochristian and Byzantine ivories, including the famous *Harbaville triptych* (138) from the middle of the 10th century, in which Christ, the Virgin, St John the Baptist, apostles and saints are portrayed in the precise, conventional style of the monuments of that period; the *Crowning of the Virgin* (139) and the charming *Virgin* from the treasure of the Sainte-Chapelle, with its slightly affected elegance; high quality pieces of Mediaeval gold and silver-work such as (shown in the room reserved for the Baron Adolphe de Rothschild donation) the triptych shrine, in silver-gilt, from the Abbay of Floreffe (Belgium) (1254) or the *reliquary arm casket of St Louis of Toulouse* in crystal and enamelled silver-gilt, supposedly executed in Naples in 1337; Roman and Gothic hollowed-out enamels, such as the *Resurrection* shoulder-plate (140) from a workshop in the Meuse (about 1175-1180) or the *Death of the Virgin* plate, from a workshop in the Limousin (about 1200-1210); painted enamels of the 16th century, including those of Léonard Limosin, the great Limoges enameller, and specially his portrait of *Anne de Montmorency* (143) framed with the emblems of his post as High Commissioner; Hispano-Moresque, Italian and French ceramics of the 14th, 15th and 16th centuries; Mediaeval bronzes, the oldest being the famous equestrian statue known as that of Charlemagne (9th century?) (141) from the treasure of the cathedral of Metz, and more numerous ones from the Italian Renaissance, specially by the Padovian master, Andrea Riccio (142); and finally tapestries, including the *Virgin in Glory*, woven in Brussels in 1485 and above all, the splendid series of *Maximilien's Hunts* executed in the same town in about 1530 from designs by Bernard van Orley.

The rooms on the first floor of the North Wing of the Square Courtyard contain examples of French furniture and decoration from the 16th century to the Restoration. The pieces of cabinetwork, tapestry,

141. Statuette, known as that of Charlemagne, bronze (9th cen.)

142. Andrea Riccio Orpheus (known as Arion), bronze (ap.1500)

143. Léonard Limosin The High Constable Montmorency, enamel painted on copper (1566)

ceramic, gold and silver-work, clockwork, are all outstanding and constitute a series of ensembles presented in chronological order, so that each illustrates a given period, a particular style, or the work of some artist (A.-Ch. Boulle, Ch. Cressent, J.F. Oeben, M. Carlin, J.H. Riesener...) (144-150).

144. Bed of Marshal d'Effiat
(Louis XIII period)

145. Writing-table, known as that of Vergennes, by Pierre II Migeon and J. Dubois (ap.1750)

146. Armchair from Marie-Antoinette's inner closet at Saint-Cloud, by Sené, Vallois and Hauré (1787)

147. August (detail)
Tapestry from the series "Maximilien's Hunts"
Brussels (ap.1530)

148. Light bracket, bronze-gilt,
attributed to Duplessis (Louis XV period)

Below left
149. Napoleon I's washstand in the Tuileries

151. Snuff-box
presented by Louis XV to Le Fort,
Syndic of Geneva,
Gowers, Paris (1726-1727)

150. Lyre-shaped clock,
Sèvres china and bronze-gilt,
Coteaux enamels (Louis XVI period)

152. Chest, Japanese lacquer and bronze-gilt,
by Martin Carlin (ap.1780)

Layout:
Bruno Pfäffli

Photography:
Réunion des musées nationaux, Paris

Photocomposition:
Union Linotypiste, Paris

Printing:
Imprimerie moderne du Lion, Paris

ISBN 2.7118.0040.7

Printed in France